Jim Abbott

by Mark Stewart

ACKNOWLEDGMENTS
The editors wish to thank Jim Abbott for his cooperation in preparing this book.
Thanks also to Integrated Sports International for their assistance.

PHOTO CREDITS
All photos courtesy AP/Wide World Photos, Inc. except the following:

California Angels – Cover, 4 top left, 5, bottom right, 6, 25 top right, 29
The Flint Journal, Flint, Michigan – 8, 12
University of Michigan – 15, 24 top left
Reuters/Bettmann – 11
Mark Stewart – 48

STAFF
Project Coordinator: John Sammis, Cronopio Publishing
Series Design Concept: The Sloan Group
Design and Electronic Page Makeup: Jaffe Enterprises, and
        Digital Communications Services, Inc.

LIBRARY OF CONGRESS CATALOGING-IN-PUBLICATION DATA
Stewart, Mark.
    Jim Abbott / by Mark Stewart.
        p. cm. – [Grolier all-pro biographies]
    Includes index.
    Summary: A biography of the California Angels pitcher who has only one hand.
    ISBN 0-516-20152-2 [lib. binding] – 0-516-26006-5 [pbk.]
    1. Abbott, Jim, 1967-   – Juvenile literature. 2. Baseball players—United States—Biography—
Juvenile literature. 3. Physically handicapped baseball players—United States—Biography—
Juvenile literature [1. Abbott, Jim, 1967-   . 2. Baseball players. 3. Physically-handicapped.]
I. Title. II. Series.
GV865.A26S84 1996
796.357'092—dc20
[B]   96-33792
                                                                                                CIP
                                                                                                 AC

Grolier ALL-PRO Biographies™

Jim Abbott

by
Mark Stewart

CHILDREN'S PRESS®
A Division of Grolier Publishing
New York • London • Hong Kong • Sydney
Danbury, Connecticut

Contents

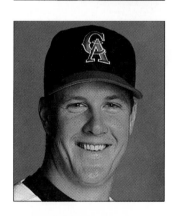

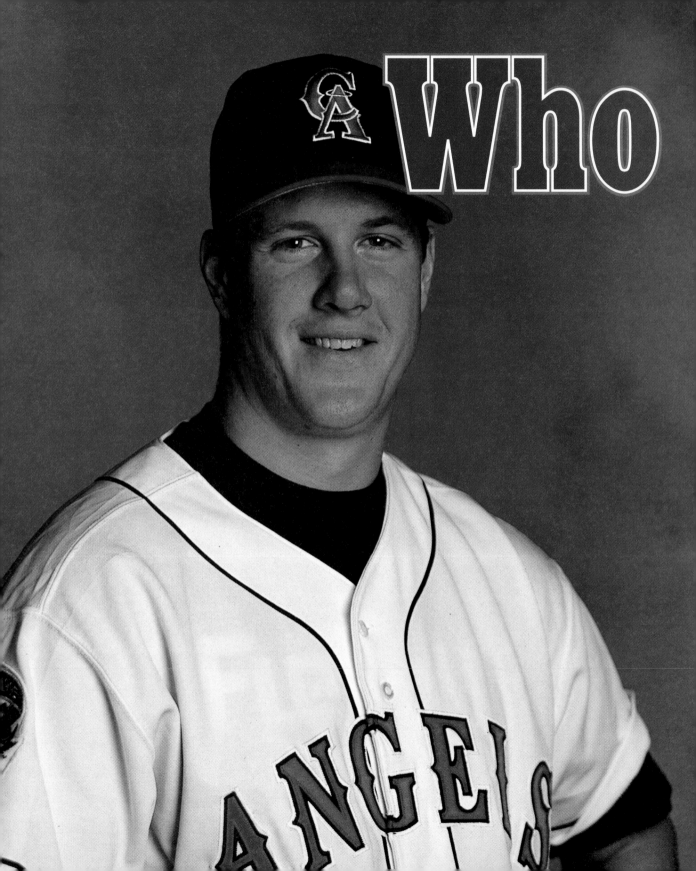

Who

Am I?

Y ou know how good it feels to be told you're special? Well, for most of my life I got that same feeling when people treated me the same as everyone else. That's because there is something different about me. Some people call it a handicap, although it has never stopped me from doing what I want to do—and that includes fulfilling my dream of pitching in the major leagues. Yet as far back as I can remember, someone always seemed to be telling me not to set my goals too high. It just wasn't common sense. My name is Jim Abbott, and this is my story . . . "

"Some people call it a handicap, but it has never stopped me from fulfilling my dream."

Growing Up

I n 1967, Mike and Kathy Abbott were a young couple anxiously awaiting the birth of their first child. When their son finally arrived, he was born without a right hand. But Mike and Kathy did not allow themselves to be sad or angry. The way they saw it, their baby, Jim, was beautiful and healthy. They would accept him, and as a family, they would overcome his disability.

When Jim was very young, he was fitted with a prosthesis, a device intended to perform some functions of his missing hand. Other children thought the claw-

Jim began playing little league when he was eleven years old.

When he was young, Jim was a big fan of the Detroit Tigers. Two of his favorite players were pitcher Mickey Lolich (left) and hitting star Al Kaline (right).

like prosthesis looked strange. Some kids called him cruel names, like "The Crab" and "Captain Hook." After a while Jim, decided to stop wearing the prosthetic hand, and his parents went along with his wishes. Jim remembers, "I was born with the challenge of having only one hand. I dealt with it by trying to be a little more outgoing and join as many different activities and get involved in as many sports as I could. That really helped. I never thought to myself, 'Oh wow, I only have one hand.' I just found a way to do the same things other kids did."

Jim's father was a big baseball fan, and soon Jim became interested in the game. The Abbotts lived in Flint, Michigan, so they watched the Detroit Tigers on television and rooted for players such as Al Kaline, Willie Horton, Mickey Lolich, and Bill Freehan. Jim wanted to play baseball with the other children, but he realized that fielding and throwing would be complicated with just one hand. After many months of practice, Jim learned to catch and throw quickly and smoothly. He began to forget that he had only one hand.

Jim played third base and the outfield on his Little League team and did very well. He was a good fielder and had a strong arm. One day, the team's starting pitcher felt ill, so the coach asked Jim to fill in. Jim shocked everyone—he took the mound and pitched a no-hitter!

On the baseball field and in school, Jim's friends found that he was really no different from anyone else. He collected baseball cards and listened to music. He liked to read, but he also liked to watch television. In school, he was good at science and not so good at math.

Jim recalls, "I considered schoolwork a challenge and took great pride in getting good grades. Even so, today I look back and regret not learning more when I had the chance. I wish I had learned geography a little better, because when I watch the news now I never know where anything is. You don't think about these things when you're young, but they turn out to be very important. As for reading, I'd have to say that it is not only enjoyable—it's essential."

Jim really began to enjoy school in the third grade. His

teacher that year was Mr. Clarkson, who always seemed to have extra time to spend with the students. Before he became a teacher, Mr. Clarkson worked for NASA in the 1960s, when astronauts had first landed on the moon. Jim found Mr. Clarkson's stories about his NASA experiences fascinating.

At home, Jim's father encouraged his interest in sports. But one rule was clear: schoolwork should always come first. Before Jim went to school each morning, his father would tell him to be a leader, to think for himself, and to live his life the way he wanted to live it. To this day, Jim lives by those words.

As Jim got older, his parents could see that he was a good athlete. They secretly hoped he would take up soccer (a game in which nobody uses their hands) so Jim would not be at a disadvantage. But Jim wanted to play baseball, football, and basketball. His coaches and teammates admired him for his ability to succeed in these "hands-on" sports, but they assumed that he would eventually find these games too difficult.

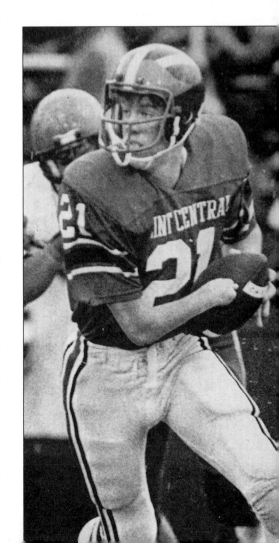

In addition to baseball, Jim was an excellent football player in high school.

Jim fooled everyone. He became the star quarterback and punter for his high-school team, and he led the Flint Central Indians to the state semifinals in his senior year. He was also the top scorer on his intramural basketball team. And, of course, Jim was a terrific pitcher in baseball. As a senior, Jim struck out an average of two batters an inning, and he allowed an average of only two hits per game. His record during his final two seasons was 20 wins and 5 losses.

Jim was an outstanding high-school pitcher.

Some opponents attempted to take advantage of Jim by bunting the ball and forcing him to field it. They thought that because Jim had only one hand, he was a poor fielder. One team tried bunting on Jim eight times in a row before they finally learned their lesson. Jim could actually field bunts faster than most pitchers with two hands, and he threw out the batter almost every time! When Jim was not pitching, he played the outfield. As a one-handed hitter, he learned to hit the ball between the fielders so well that one season his batting average was over .400.

During his senior year in high school in 1985, the Toronto Blue Jays chose Jim in the June amateur draft. They then asked him to come to Tiger Stadium when the team traveled to Detroit that summer. A few hours before game time, Toronto scouts and coaches gathered around the mound and watched Jim pitch to an unknown rookie by the name of Cecil Fielder. The scouts were so impressed that they offered Jim $50,000 to sign a contract. But Jim had other ideas. The University of Michigan had offered him a scholarship, and to play for the Wolverines was Jim's lifelong dream. He thanked Toronto for its offer and politely turned down the Blue Jays.

College

Jim Abbott made the Wolverine varsity team in his freshman season and quickly began making headlines. In his first home game, Jim combined with Scott Kamieniecki to pitch a no-hitter. Years later, Scott and Jim would be teammates on the New York Yankees. By the end of his first college season, Jim had six victories, including the win that gave Michigan the Big 10 Conference title. As a sophomore, Jim was even better, going 11 and 3, and leading the team to another Big 10 championship.

In 1985, Jim accepted a baseball scholarship from the University of Michigan.

Years

Jim throws a pitch against Cuba as a member of Team U.S.A.

Life was beginning to change for Jim. Whenever he pitched, huge numbers of fans showed up. Many in the crowd had physical disabilities. Although Jim always said he was "just another student," deep down he knew that these people viewed him as an inspiration. He always went out of his way to say hello and talk with his fans before games. By the end of his sophomore year, Jim was beginning to receive national attention. Newspapers and magazines were calling him a "One-Armed Wonder," and there were television crews at almost all of his starts.

That summer at the 1987 Pan American Games, Jim became an international sensation. He pitched Team U.S.A. to victory over Cuba's powerhouse squad in Havana, Cuba. Each time he walked to the mound, the fans gave him a huge ovation.

When the game was over, Cuban ruler Fidel Castro asked Jim for his autograph. That fall he was awarded the Golden Spikes Award as the country's finest college baseball player. A few months later, he edged David Robinson and Janet Evans for the Sullivan Award—the highest honor an amateur athlete can receive.

Despite all of the awards and attention, Jim was able to stay focused on his studies. As a college junior, he was voted team MVP, Big 10 Conference Player of the Year, and was honored as an All-American.

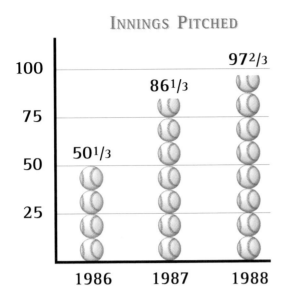

INNINGS PITCHED

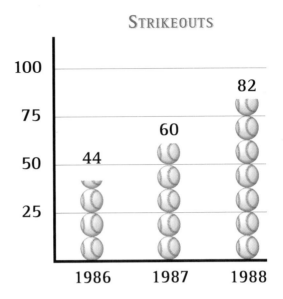

STRIKEOUTS

With a 26 and 8 college record and a fastball that hummed past hitters at 94 miles per hour, Jim was rated among the top pitching prospects in America. In June 1988, the California Angels chose Jim with their first pick in the draft. Before he joined the Angels, Jim joined Team U.S.A. again, this time for a trip to the Olympics. In Seoul, South Korea, Jim took the mound in the gold medal game against Japan. Although he knew immediately that he did not have his best stuff that day, Jim pitched a courageous ballgame and won 5 to 3. He still considers winning the gold medal to be the biggest thrill of his career.

Road to

For the great majority of pitchers, there is one road to the major leagues: the minor leagues. When Jim Abbott signed with California, only nine other pitchers had jumped directly to the big leagues since the baseball draft began in 1965. When spring training opened in 1989, no one was expecting Jim to be the tenth. Of course, that did not stop the press from following his every move. There were dozens of television, newspaper, and magazine reporters in camp looking for another Jim Abbott story. He even had to turn down three book deals and a big-money offer to film a movie of his life. Jim knew that there would be a lot of commotion surrounding him, but this was getting ridiculous.

Finally Jim got to throw his first pitch in an exhibition game. His fastball exploded into the catcher's mitt, and his slider danced down and in on right-handed hitters. In three scoreless innings, Jim gave up a couple of harmless singles

the Pros

and struck out four men. He had remarkable command of his pitches for a young left-hander, and he demonstrated the poise of a veteran on the mound.

Every time he pitched that spring he looked great, and fans speculated that Jim had a chance to go to the Angels' AAA team at Edmonton. This would be just one step from the big leagues. But when the final cuts were made, Jim was still on the Angels' major-league roster. Not only did he make the team, he was in the starting rotation! Not surprisingly, Jim Abbott was the hottest story in baseball.

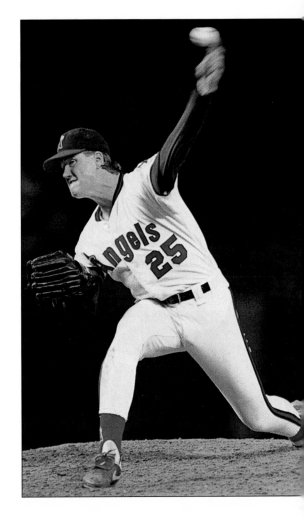

Rookie pitcher Jim Abbott records his first major-league complete game and his first shutout.

The Story

Jim Abbott had his ups and downs as a major-league rookie, but when the season was over he had won 12 games. His success was a big reason why the Angels improved from 75 wins in 1988 to 91 wins in 1989. In 1991, Jim had his breakout season. He won 18, lost 11, and turned in a 2.89 ERA. At an age when most players are still in the minor leagues, Jim finished third in the Cy Young Award voting.

In 1989, Jim's 12 victories set a record for rookies who had jumped directly to the major leagues.

Continues

Jim leaps to snare
a high bouncer.

In 1992, Jim threw well again and lowered his ERA to 2.77. But California's hitters failed to support the team's pitchers, and Jim's record sank to 7–15. That winter the Angels had to make a blockbuster trade to get some offense. They traded Jim to the New York Yankees for first baseman J. T. Snow and two pitchers.

As a member of the Yankees in 1993, Jim pitched a no-hitter against the powerful Cleveland Indians. The following year, he had a 9 and 8 record and helped New York open a solid lead in the American League's Eastern Division. But Jim missed his chance to pitch in the playoffs when a labor dispute between players and owners led to cancellation of the season in August.

In 1993, Jim joined
Paul O'Neill (left) and
Spike Owen on the
New York Yankees.

Jim went 6–4 during a half-season stint with the Chicago White Sox in 1995.

Jim decided to test the free agent market after the 1994 season, and he signed with the Chicago White Sox. The team was favored to win the A.L. Central in 1995, but pitching problems held the Sox back. By mid-season they were out of the running, although Jim played well. Many teams contacted Chicago asking if he was available. Realizing they could not catch the hot Cleveland Indians, the White Sox traded Jim to . . . the Angels! Happy to return to the city where he started, Jim won five more games to help the Angels tie for the division title.

Timeline

1985:
Enrolls at the
University of
Michigan

1988: Pitches Team
U.S.A. to a gold medal
in the 1988 Olympics
in Seoul, South Korea

1987:
Leads Team
U.S.A. to
silver medal
at Pan
American
Games

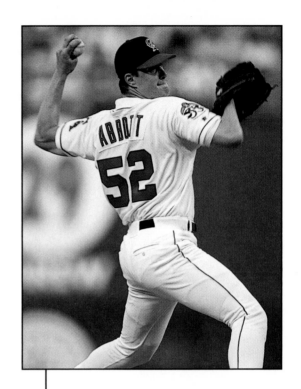

1989: Joins the California Angels without spending a day in the minors; wins 12 games as a rookie

1995: Starts 17 games for the Chicago White Sox and then is traded back to the California Angels

1993: Traded to the New York Yankees; throws a no-hitter on September 4

Game

The chilly relations between the United States and Cuba melted away during the 1987 Pan Am games, when Cuban fans gave Jim a standing ovation every time he took the mound.

The leap from college ball directly into the majors required Jim to make one important adjustment: he had to learn how to pitch inside to right-handed power hitters.

Action!

> "The part of my game that I am most proud of is my fielding. It is also the part I work hardest on."

J im went 8 and 1 with a 2.55 ERA for the 1988 U.S. Olympic Team.

J im gives credit to his pitching coach with the Angels. "Marcel Lachemann taught me how to pitch—he's an incredible coach."

"My most embarrassing moment was getting beaten 7–0 by Seattle in my first major-league game."

Jim made headlines in a 1989 spring training game when he hit a one-handed triple off pitcher Rick Reuschel.

Jim looks over historic Yankee Stadium. Jim's trade from Anaheim to New York was unpopular with Angels fans.

California fans never forgave the Angels for trading Jim to the Yankees after the 1992 season. When highlights of his 1993 no-hitter were shown on the Anaheim Stadium scoreboard, Angels fans gave him a standing ovation.

Although Jim is not as superstitious as most ballplayers, he admits that he was wearing his "lucky" pants the day he hurled his no-hitter.

When Jim returned to the Angels in 1995, outfielder Jim Edmonds was wearing his old number—25. Jim decided to take number 52, which is 25 backwards!

Dealing

For the past decade, Jim Abbott has had to deal with something much tougher than the day-to-day difficulty of life with just one hand. He has had to put up with the day-to-day pressure of being interviewed, photographed, and mobbed everywhere he goes. At first, he tried to convince everyone that there was nothing special about him. But finally he came to realize that whether people viewed him as an inspiration or a curiosity, he would always be in the spotlight.

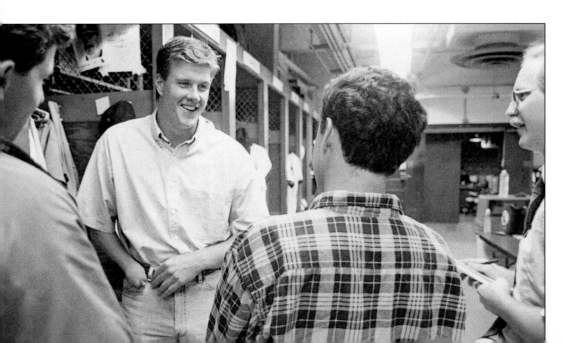

Wherever he goes, Jim is interviewed by the media.

With It

Jim's courage and friendliness have made him a fan favorite.

"I've been blessed with a pretty good left arm and a not-so-good right arm. But I don't think of myself as being handicapped—I mean, my hand has not kept me from doing anything I wanted to do. However, it's something that's always going to be part of my story. I understand that and I'm not going to run away from it. Ideally, though, I'd prefer to be recognized for pitching well and nothing else."

HOW DOES

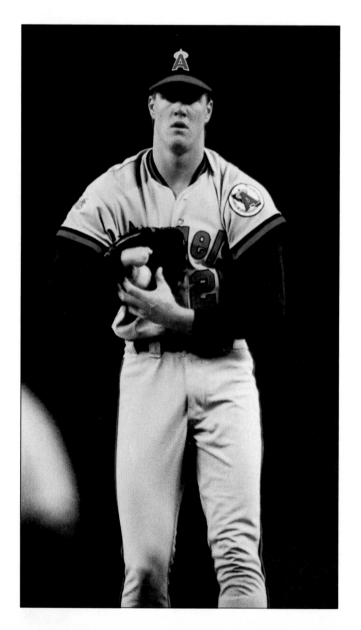

Jim Abbott learned to throw and field with the same hand so long ago that now he does not even think about it. He keeps his glove on the end of his right arm when he winds up and throws to the plate, then quickly slips his hand into the glove after his follow-through. When Jim scoops up a grounder, he jams his glove into the crook of his right

Jim transfers the ball from his glove to his throwing hand.

He Do It?

Jim prepares to flip the ball to first base after making a nice fielding play. Jim is one of the best fielding pitchers in the majors.

elbow, plucks the ball out with his left hand, and then throws to first base. It happens so fast that each step is hard to see. In fact, because Jim has worked so long on this motion, he fields his position better than most pitchers in the majors!

The Grind

Jim Abbott understands and accepts the demands of being one of the most well-known people in sports, and he lives up to the responsibilities that come with being an inspiration to so many millions of people. Still, he has never gotten used to the time away from his family. Also, no matter how many people tell him how great he is, he still must go out and prove it every five days.

"The hardest thing is always trying to be your best. There are times when you're tired and other times when maybe you don't

After giving up a home run, Jim gathers his confidence to continue pitching well.

believe in yourself. That's when you have to stick it out and draw on all the confidence that you have, deep down beneath all the doubts and worries."

Jim knows he can't win every game he starts, so he tries to learn from his poor performances.

Say What?

Here's what people are saying about Jim Abbott:

"I never cease to be amazed by Jim. He's in a class by himself."

—Doug Rader,
former California Angels manager

"You don't have to ask Jim what he can't do—just sit back and watch what he *can* do."

—Rick Turner,
former California Angels teammate

"His fastball is overpowering, and he seems like he's in total control out there."

—Lance Parrish, former California Angels catcher

"Not only did we get a quality pitcher, we got an old friend back."

—*Richard Brown,*
California Angels president

"He's got a great makeup, great desire. He wants to win."

—*Marcel Lachemann, California Angels manager*

"Just when you think Abbott has surpassed all rational expectations, he gets better."

—*Tom Boswell, sportswriter*

"His mechanics are incredible . . . and he fields better than I do!"

—*Mike Ignasiak, Milwaukee Brewers,*
former college teammate

Career

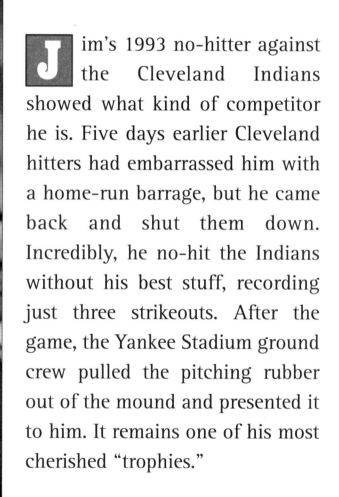

Jim's 1993 no-hitter against the Cleveland Indians showed what kind of competitor he is. Five days earlier Cleveland hitters had embarrassed him with a home-run barrage, but he came back and shut them down. Incredibly, he no-hit the Indians without his best stuff, recording just three strikeouts. After the game, the Yankee Stadium ground crew pulled the pitching rubber out of the mound and presented it to him. It remains one of his most cherished "trophies."

Jim tips his cap to the Yankee Stadium crowd after pitching his no-hitter on Sept. 4, 1993.

Highlights

Jim's 12 wins in 1989 established a new record. No pitcher who skipped the minor leagues and started his career in the majors has ever had more victories in his rookie season. The previous mark was held by Dick Ruthven, with six.

When Jim won the 1988 Sullivan Award as the nation's top amateur athlete, he became the first baseball player ever to earn this honor.

Jim's 2.89 ERA in 1991 was the best among American League left-handed starters.

During his rookie season, Hall of Famers Warren Spahn, Ernie Banks, and Bobby Doerr asked Jim for his autograph.

Jim is not baseball's first one-handed pitcher. More than 100 years ago, Hugh Daily won 73 games in six seasons, and once struck out 13 men in a game.

Jim was the ace pitcher for the 1988 U. S. Olympic team. But it was his bare-handed fielding play against Japan that saved the final game and clinched the gold medal for Team U.S.A.

Reaching

Jim Abbott is involved with many charities, including Amigos de los Niños (Friends of the Children). He has donated more than $100,000 to this organization, which helps needy children with and without disabilities.

Jim also works with the Little League Challenger Division to get physically challenged kids more involved in baseball. Jim's biggest impact, however, is on the thousands of kids he never meets—the thousands who are inspired to overcome their disabilities. One such person was David Goulding, who also was born with just one hand. After reading of Jim's success, David tried out for his local Pop Warner football team. The Atlanta boy not only made the team, he caught four passes in the 1987 championship game! David later went on to Brigham Young University, where he became a star pitcher, just like Jim.

Jim gets directly involved with the Little League Challenger Division.

Out

Numbers

Name: James Anthony Abbott

Weight: 210 pounds

Born: September 19, 1967

Uniform Number: 52

Height: 6' 3"

College: University of Michigan

Jim and teammates Mark Langston and Chuck Finely were the three winningest lefties in the American League in 1991. No other team in history has had the league's three most victorious southpaws in one season.

Year	Team	Games	Wins	Losses	Winning Pct.	ERA	SO
1989	California Angels	29	12	12	.500	3.92	115
1990	California Angels	33	10	14	.417	4.51	105
1991	California Angels	34	18	11	.621	2.89	158
1992	California Angels	29	7	15	.318	2.77	130
1993	New York Yankees	32	11	14	.440	4.37	95
1994	New York Yankees	24	9	8	.529	4.55	90
1995	Chicago White Sox/ California Angels	30	11	8	.579	3.70	86
TOTALS		211	78	82	.488	3.77	779

What If...

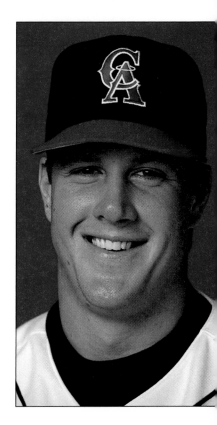

At every level I reached in sports, someone was there to tell me that this was as high as I would get. What if one of those people had been right? What if I did not have the talent to make it to the majors? I always set my goals high, but I made sure I knew what the stepping stones were to reach those goals. Most importantly, I also knew what the consequences were if I got knocked off along the way. That is why I chose to attend college instead of going directly into professional baseball—a chance for a free education was worth more than any bonus I could have been offered. If I were not playing baseball today, I might be a landscape architect, or perhaps work for the National Parks Service—something where I could be outdoors. The important thing is that my education would have enabled me to do anything I wanted to do."

Glossary

CURIOSITY an unusual object or person that arouses the interest of others

ESSENTIAL necessary and most important

COMMOTION fuss, noise, excitement

CONFIDENCE a feeling of trust and belief in oneself

CONSEQUENCES the result of an action

SCHOLARSHIP money given to a student to help pay for schooling

SPECULATED thought up reasons for; guessed at

VETERAN one who has had a lot of experience

WORK ETHIC a high moral standard maintained while trying to reach a set goal

IMPACT a strong, immediate effect

IRONICALLY surprisingly; with a twist of fate

OVATION enthusiastic applause

POISE the ability to present oneself in a cool, calm, and confident manner

PURSUIT the act of working toward a goal

RATIONAL sensible; reasonable

REQUIRED called for; necessary

Index

About The Author

Mark Stewart grew up in New York City in the 1960s and 1970s—when the Mets, Jets, and Knicks all had championship teams. As a child, Mark read everything about sports he could lay his hands on. Today, he is one of the busiest sportswriters around. Since 1990, he has written close to 500 sports stories for kids, including profiles on more than 200 athletes, past and present. A graduate of Duke University, Mark served as senior editor of *Racquet*, a national tennis magazine, and was managing editor of *Super News*, a sporting goods industry newspaper. He is the author of every Grolier All-Pro Biography.